LIT BLUE SKY FALLING

poems by

Meg Files

Finishing Line Press
Georgetown, Kentucky

LIT BLUE SKY FALLING

*For my sisters, Sally and Susan,
wonderful companions on our journey,
with great admiration and love*

Copyright © 2019 by **Meg Files**
ISBN 978-1-64662-017-3 First Edition
All rights reserved under International and Pan-American Copyright Conventions. No part of this book may be reproduced in any manner whatsoever without written permission from the publisher, except in the case of brief quotations embodied in critical articles and reviews.

ACKNOWLEDGMENTS

Grateful acknowledgment is made to the editors of the following literary magazines and anthologies where these poems originally appeared:

Cloudbank: "Independence Day," "With My Father at JJ's Barber Shop," and "Aurora Borealis"
Driftfish: A Zoomorphic Anthology: "Penguin Parade"
Galapagos Triptych (Imago Press): "Embarkation," "The Blue-Footed Booby," "El Solitario George," "Origin of Species," "Found in Translation: Snapshots"
Miramar: "Powdered Milk"
The Blue Guitar: "Aspen Fire"
The Burden of Light: Poems on Illness and Loss: "Post-Procedure"
Writing Out of the Darkness: An Anthology of Poetry by Refugees in Transition: "Lit Blue Sky Falling"
A Walk with Nature anthology: "Sublunary"
Panoply: "Bad Mammo"

Publisher: Leah Maines
Editor: Christen Kincaid
Cover Art: Monika Rossa
Author Photo: Picture People Studio
Cover Design: Elizabeth Maines McCleavy

Printed in the USA on acid-free paper.
Order online: www.finishinglinepress.com
  also available on amazon.com

Author inquiries and mail orders:
Finishing Line Press
P. O. Box 1626
Georgetown, Kentucky 40324
U. S. A.

Table of Contents

1

Embarkation 1
The Blue-Footed Booby 2
El Solitario George 4
Origin of Species 5
Found in Translation: Snapshots 7

2

Powdered Milk 9
Aspen Fire 11
Mongolian Dust Storm 13
Post-Procedure 14
Penguin Parade 16
Bad Mammo 18
With My Father at JJ's Barber Shop 19
Graduation 21
Transmutation 22
Independence Day 2017 24
Lit Blue Sky Falling 25

3

How to Travel with Your Twin Sisters 27
Sublunary 29
Translation of Bones 31
Aurora Borealis 33
Skald 34

EMBARKATION

> *The real voyage of discovery consists not in seeking new landscapes but in having new eyes.*
> —Marcel Proust

We believe we are prepared for this
trip: all-terrain shoes, tiny clothesline,
mesh-sided shirts, new underwear,
Columbia shorts, everything cute enough
for each other. At the Quito airport,
the driver holds a sign—Sally Jean
Susan Lee Margaret Kay—expecting
six instead of three with middle names.
At Guayllambamba we are given bumpy
green fruit with insides like cooked fish.
Each rod of flesh holds a long black
seed. We taste this chirimoya but not
the cuy (a pretty name for guinea pig).
The guide poses us at the equator, where
we weigh two pounds less. A day of calm
volcanoes, a trek past an outdoor mass—
Then sings my soul—to Peguche waterfall
where boys tumble below the celebrants,

and we come to Guachala, oldest hacienda
in the country, where we need to be.
For dinner we are led past all others
to a small table behind a giant bread oven
as if the staff can see our weight of secrets.

We are brought wine. Ready to go
forward, we cast ourselves back—*This
is what I saw, this is my sealed pain.*
Here and here and here are our slick
black seeds, and we open our white grief
flesh and our eyes are washed new. Later
in my room I have a fire and Agua Mineral
(*un milagro de la naturaleza*). Outside
the wind in the eucalyptus is the ocean. Now
we sisters, doubled, and lighter, are prepared
to make our journey to the strange islands.

THE BLUE-FOOTED BOOBY

> *It would appear that the birds of this archipelago, not having as yet learnt that man is a more dangerous animal than the tortoise or the Amblyrhynchus, disregard him...*
> —Charles Darwin

We found the first blue-footed boobies
ourselves, no guide, as if we were first
to swim Tortuga Bay (which would not
have a name), scull below the cooled
lava rocks, and discover these birds who,
having no memory of us, are indifferent.

Their webbed feet make me think of my
blue swim fins, but we remind them
of nothing, not the Spanish sailors who
laughed at the bobos, nor the British ship's
hatch where once they perched. I suppose
they know their bills are pale matching blue.

The next day on Seymour Island, baby
blue-footed boobies wait in their bare-
ground nests within guano rings for
mothers to come home with fish. Their feet
are powdered white, their down plump
white. The parents still remember to gather

twigs for a nest but forget why. The man
in the i love boobies tee-shirt cries out—
there on the trail is the display of a fallen
chick, stiff and flat, open-beaked head
on a rock pillow. The feet are curled
and gray (human note: never to be blue).

Observe survival of the fittest: the guide
is matter-of-fact. When, now and then, two
eggs in one nest hatch, the babies grow
for eight weeks and then the first-hatched
pecks the sibling out of the home circle
where no one cares. The guide is reverent:

here no mass starvation but should tragedy
befall the older, the younger saves

the generation. (What kind of mother, we
mutter, how Cain and Abel.) We were not
there, so the birds do not remember
us. What is cruelty, what is beauty, without

memory? I remember the brown-winged
booby, its blue legs inserted into its white body
its pale blue beak sideways (so for a moment
I believe its right eye sees my human form)
and the way it launches itself straight
from the guano-ed rock into the water.

EL SOLITARIO GEORGE

> *They seemed newly crawled forth from beneath the foundations of the world.*
> —Herman Melville

Last tortoise found on Isla Pinta, he lives
now at the Charles Darwin Research
Station. We see his winsome face
on a placard on his pen but only
the back of his real self in the foliage.
An old guidebook says he "may be
allowed" to breed with a close
genetic relation. Now he cohabits with
two females from Wolf Volcano. Once
his love life was tourist gossip. Once
a $10,000 reward awaited the one who

found a female of his subspecies. In the next
pen over, females without males urinate to
make mud and dig with their back legs to create
nests for eggs they will not lay. They raise and
rock their plodding bodies. Their faces look
determined and thickly sad. Next to them are
the males, also former pets who must not
breed so island species won't be mixed. They
are huge as boulders, a century and a half
of querulous baggy necks and broken shells.

The next day, the tortoises in the wild
seem noble, not sad at all. Is George truly
lonesome? He will not take the Wolf Volcano
offerings. He is only 60 or 70, young enough.
Beside him, the females paddle back legs
in the muck they have made and the old
males doze open-eyed in their concrete ponds
beside the feeding platform strewn
with leftovers. And George, last of his kind,
saves himself finally to crawl back alone
beneath the cradle of the earth. The end.

ORIGIN OF SPECIES

> ... *both in space and time, we seem to be brought somewhat near to that great fact—that mystery of mysteries—the first appearance of new beings on this earth.*
> —Charles Darwin

1.
Before the voyage Darwin turned away
from medicine when he witnessed
the agony of surgery. On the islands he
observed thirteen species of finch, each
with a different beak adapted to different
seeds. And so it goes. He believed
in a Designer until he found natural
selection, until his little daughter died.
What is faith? grace notes? curlicues?
Now on the islands, my sisters dispense
seasick pills and would tell old Darwin
about genomes. "The sight of a feather
in a peacock's tail, whenever I gaze at it,
makes me sick," Darwin told his son.
For what had such deep-dyed glory to do
with natural selection? What is mystery?
a tease? disbelief? Yes, yes, I know
evolution has no intent. Is it enough to see?

2.
God did not allow suffering before the fall,
say the Creationists, and the animals
were safe from human hunger. And so
it goes: sin came into the world, and
death and fossils followed. In our world
grace dies every day, as do men whose
singular voices bend the air and young
mothers and crashed children and poets
whose words are phosphorescence in a dark
sea. In the islands, our dead mother rides
the panga from boat to land with my sisters
and me. *Pay attention, you girls.* All
are extinct, each creature its own species,
unadapted, unselected. And you, and we,
adapted, selected, witness the fall, and fall.

3.
We go to these islands to believe
it is possible to isolate ourselves.
Death cannot swim nor spring
from the volcano nor descend.
We walk among these iguanas,
these frigates, sea lions, finches,
these tortoises with Charles.
We record field notes. We are
of the species. Jesus probably
walked on foggy Galilee's surface
ice, but here we might be sore
amazed when our mother treads
back to us across the clear Pacific
blue. A distance from the boat
are breeching whales, tails, then
whole bodies, in beauty beyond
words. We are new beings on
this earth. Is it enough to see?

FOUND IN TRANSLATION: SNAPSHOTS

> ... *one is astonished here at the amount of creative force, if such an expression may be used, displayed on these small, barren, and rocky islands...*
> —Charles Darwin

The guide directs our eyes. *Here we have plate-billed mountain toucan. Here you see epiphytes,* parasites that love the host. *You will see. You will see.*

Here we are at Bellavista Reserve, one by one taken beneath umbrella leaves. To make the cloud forest, *the wind comes and cherishes the mountains.*

The hacienda menu instructs us: *order cuy 24 hours with anticipation.* We choose *fish of grilled. Here you see extinct Volcan Cayambe,* no human in sight to dare it.

Darwin himself directed us on his journey: We will turn now to the terrestrial species. I will describe the habits of the tortoise. We will now turn to the order of reptiles.

The cones of Bartolemé Island display their proud lava spills as if in cheerful competition. Here you see mighty women hold boulders above their heads.

Diving with air in their lungs, the sea lions here bark underwater. The marine iguana has two sexual organs but can use only one at a time. Which leg will he pick up?

The male frigate inflates his red sac—oh love, come—his heart a ridiculous balloon on his chest. Sally Lightfoot crabs need black lava rocks under their primary splendor.

Here we are in a lava tube, the lit green entrance to the world behind us. In this

one you see us grinning from the boat's
patched orange life buoy, hands to eyes.

Sharks cruise near the beach and no one
minds. Children run into the keen water
and adults enter ankle to shin to thigh.
Land iguanas' legs are beaded in gold.

We will turn now from the islands' salt
bush and lava cactus. The guide back
in the country will say, *the leaves are
proud.* And we see they have turned red.

But first we climb onto a little canopied
outboard. The pilot warns, *the water is
very moving.* For hours the craft slams
our bones into the knotted cobalt sea.

My sisters give pills to the men hiding
their seasickness behind cloths held
to mouths. Some are prepared to leap.
But no, for *the water here is profound.*

Here you see me kissing the dock. We
have walked the teeming barren islands,
taken soundings, crossed the profound
waters. We have seen: we have yet to see.

POWDERED MILK

My first husband's life went
on after I ran with
the baby, I learn from
the obit. Another

wife, dead now, two girls and
a boy with the same name
he gave to my son, armed
service, perhaps what turned

him around, as they say.
His spent father, his ma
who made me drink powdered
milk, gone. Odd: just today,

before this knowledge, in
the drugstore I sniffed that
certain brand of powder
I could not, pregnant, bear,

and my gut curdled. There
are those who believe I
have always waited for
that upraised hand. Long since,

I guessed they could not buy
those gallons of cold whole
milk I, gravid, craved. In
the photo he is still

young, in uniform, no
one I know, newly then
in control of his hands.
I want to know what killed

that boy. In my desert
beneath the swaddling of
the Milky Way, I see
a low Michigan sky.

I am frowning over
his life that ended, he
said, when I boarded that
bus, rife with my own milk.

ASPEN FIRE

For Mia Naomi, 8/8/03

In the summer of 2003, the Aspen Fire burned nearly 85,000 acres on Mount Lemmon in the Santa Catalina Mountains.

Then God said to Noah... "This is the sign of the covenant which I make between me and you and every living creature that is with you, for all the future generations: I set my bow in the cloud, and it shall be a sign of the covenant between me and the earth." —Genesis 9:12-13

From town, the Catalinas remain,
their cut into my sky. No one is
allowed up there yet, but the ruin
is revealed in newsprint black against
memory's forest. The burn should show:
We have known (if not believed) that truth
will out. That a mountain must be more
than its familiar rise from the plain.
That consequences make a lurid
cut.
    Once on Mount Lemmon: What I saw:
my young man son posed on a rock, all
the hot forest around him and him
caught within, gazing into a dim
pool. What the camera saw: a dusty
boy camouflaged on a gray boulder
backed by brown pines and pale sky—below
a bright blue pool, fringed with bright green leaves,
and in the reflection his jacket
is golden, and his hair, and his face
looks out of the blue. This water is
the doorway to a world where the known
world is drab.
    Two nights before, I dream
my son in the bedroom chair holding
a crying daughter. And so I am
right. On her birth day—though she is far
north—below the pure shape of the burned
mountain, the monsoon frees a rainbow
that catches the ghost moon and strikes just
beyond us in the desert. I ask

how it feels to hold his child, and he
says—familiar. On the fifth day I
am holding her, my tears don't wake her:
it is suddenly impossible,
all of it, biology, the whole
story. She's feisty when she's awake,
my son says. Just wait till you see her
angry.
   We need new words for her. Don't
write about dead dogs or new babies,
I tell my students. Or for god's sake
rainbows. It's all been said by better
than you, also by worse. For the fourth
generation that I know of, this
little baby toe hooks under. Now
I know, my son says when I show him,
that she's mine.
        Within every image
is the truth. Her father is the bright
boy in the pool now boiled away. She
is more than my dream of her, flesh, and
memory, as familiar as but no
more familiar than the promise
to do, or not to do. I give up
the logic of flood and fire for
that rainbow's covenant: that the known
and the scrimmed worlds wake to each other
in flesh. What remains beyond burning.

MONGOLIAN DUST STORM

This morning the Catalina Mountains
have been disappeared. Gobi Desert dust
and the fallout of Chinese industry
rode the jet stream over the entire
Pacific Ocean and took them. The air
quality index measured two hundred
seventeen microns of particulates
per cubic meter. Which I think is not
good. Those with respiratory problems
should take precautions. But scientists are
charged—for they can see the invisible
poison in the visible dust.
                                                 With no
mountains I am back in the corn, soybean
country among the spring lambs and their shorn
mothers, when shyness crossed the street, my French
horn in its black case bumped my knee, bumped it,
I didn't get the candy bar question,
male or female? and ate my Almond Joy
with nuts in a practice room alone, when
I made myself lost in books and cornfields,
and knew but did not know I knew the dam's
exposed skin, dirty tail, knowing face, when
I was the lamb.
                            So I am missing skills.
Those possessing them make storms that carry
fallout, and we should be glad of the glow,
take precautions. They don't know those who hold
to their sidewalks take in the same microns
as those who cross the street. I fear looking
down at myself and finding the old bruise
from the horn case on my right knee. The lamb
has been raised in the dirty sweet straw and
shorn, and yes the mountains will shudder back
into place. No one knows what foreign dust
we make nor how it carries. And I am
content, lost in my ingenuous life.

POST-PROCEDURE

Do not operate machinery
Do not consume alcohol
Avoid making critical decisions
until tomorrow
        And now
I see the upright salvia
cut by the slats of my blinds.
To my sisters and me what
our father planted by the back door
        the white door
was saliva. The nurse said place this
under your tongue and I found
I could not operate even my tongue.
Beneath the blinds my books stand
        even with sweet spines broken
so I may take in
        nouns. Our mother
took this test procedure
        awake uncut
by sedative or by—hope
is the word I want but more precise
        is doubt. When I raise
the blinds the smooth stutter
sends running a Gambel's quail
        plume erect.
                This year
at least this year I will
not be taken by our mother's named
cancer. Outside my open window
rise and bloom now palo verde,
        rosemary, jumping cholla,
        a school of pricklypear,
        ocotillo: all the colors in fire.
Doubt is hope dry-mouthed
        flat, brown.
If I were allowed to make
critical decisions today
        this greenfire day
I would parch the word
from the book of names, I
would decide never

to take that door
    the sure and ashen door.

PENGUIN PARADE

The fairy penguins emerge from the ocean,
their natural habitat in which, explain the guides,
they are assured and graceful. The black

clouds roll beneath the full gold moon—high
drama—and I cannot see the dark blue
and white birds slick in the blue water. I think

of how to describe for you their sudden presence
on the shore. They do not know humans
have named their beach Summerland. They

wait to gather against predators, isn't that
always the way, and begin the safety-in-numbers
waddle across the beach to their home burrows

with their mates. It's a fifty percent mate-for-life
rate, a guide says: if she fails to produce,
he moves on. The couples on the viewing

platform elbow each other. The fairy penguins
do not know they are more acceptable for being
renamed Little Penguins. Consider the cost

of redoing all the tourist brochures. In my new
hot pink scarf and striped gloves I am warm,
but I want you on the platform beside me.

The birds do look awkward, that's the repeated
word, as they waddle. Who says the real story
is the transition from sea to burrow? Consider

the cost of our missing. No photos allowed—
the flash scares the birds, is the excuse. No doubt
correct. But humans must trick humans to sit

and simply see. The birds are not "graceful"
in the ocean nor "awkward" on the land. Neither
do they parade. Sea by day, beach by dusk,

dune burrow by night: we humans should

let their blue and white truth be ours. And I do,
except for this poem, except for your absence, I do.

BAD MAMMO

Cat, dog, man gone
to bed, leaving me—no
I have left myself—
on the hearth of this waxy
desert fire with my hands
under my shirt holding
my tits. They do feel
fuller—with what seeds?
But themselves, really,
just someone's handful.
My sisters and I still hold
contests for perky. I would
say *ah the fire burns
low* (and it does, flame-
encrusted embers) but
to write it I would lose
my crossed-armed cupping
of the known breasts, so
strange now, as I pull up
my shirt, so lurid, and
throbbing in the firelight.

WITH MY FATHER AT JJ'S BARBER SHOP

> *An aged man is but a paltry thing,*
> *A tattered coat upon a stick...*
> —W.B. Yeats

Outside the strip-mall shop is a painted
barber pole and the promise: An Old
Fashion Barber. Flat tops. All Type Hair

Cuts. Seniors $9. Inside is a pale antique
pole and more prices: Haircuts with wife's
help, $25. Wives standing close to barber

telling him what to do, $40. Four men
sit draped in maroon in barber chairs,
their velco-strapped tennis shoes on rungs,

as the other old men wait beneath model
planes drifting in the ceiling fan's wind,
against a wall of photos: fighter planes

and a pair of pink shorts. The barbers are
upright with authority, trimming the white
and gray hair, straight razor for sideburns.

I am the only woman in this place of stolid
men. It's all right, my father says, you're
my caregiver. No, I say, I'm your daughter.

The draped men hold eyes down. No smiling,
little talk. "Aw just clean it up a little bit, ain't
a hell of a lot there." On a rack are *Drive!* and

Field & Stream. On the counter Marilyn
pretends to hold down her white skirt
over a subway vent. The floor is ashed

with scraps of gray and white. I witness
the facilitation of an elegant white
combover. My father asks for extra

attention to nose and ears, and it's all a paltry
thing unless, the poet says, there is singing.

The four heads in a row are molded, eyes

downcast, silent, museum pieces, isolated
from their bodies. "Best haircut I ever had,"
my father declaims, not back in his body yet.

And then I believe I hear the thick hearts
humming beneath the purple drapes, and
the four barbers whisk those noble heads.

GRADUATION

In the dark, in the jumbled line-up, I am
newly returned from a journey. Later, awake,
I understand: Retired for one semester, I am
missing graduation for the first time in 29
years, and tomorrow I will not wedding-step
with the hooded others to sit and rise as

our students make the portage across the stage,
fist-bump the dark balloon-clouded air above,
and at last, after all the words in all the sanctified
classrooms—laugh, but they were, and not only
because I do not go there now—lift their tassels
from right to left. But in the dream, the images

jostle in the line-up, as if in a dark cloakroom,
and I tell the colleagues: from across the water I sent
each of you a book or a lampshade. Your partners,
too. I was working from an old list and some
of you might not still be together. In the dream,
I step out of the dream to laugh at myself—

All across America, people are wondering, why
did I get this lampshade? Forget symbols. All
those graduations—the pomp, the tedium,
the true year's end—bob in the lapping
twilight. Here, I say, here is your book, here
is your lampshade, and I receive them.

TRANSMUTATION

for Nancy

Here I am on this exotic island that is only
home to its citizens. On the boat, I stay
aboard for the second dive, freezing in my
inadequate wetsuit. So the shop owner back
on shore doesn't know that I overhear him
radioing to the boat captain: "Help out that
new older woman through the surf, she looks
frail." "Wait!" I say. "Is he talking about me?

Me?" On the first dive, I tried to join the school
of my favorite blue chromis, but they were
not having me. Also present: a spotted eagle
ray, the biggest nurse shark ever, my nemesis
the green moray, smiling blue tangs, angelfish.
Back home, my friend has had her diagnosis
but won't ruin my vacation by telling. Nothing
was exotic to her in the world, only true, only

home. When I return, she says: I only want
to have fun with friends. She is smiling, she
is patting her dogs. But first, I am diving on
the underwater sculpture park: lifesize casts
of children in a circle, the lost correspondent
at his desk and typewriter, a man on a bike.
From land to sea, they are now reef, with
exotic faces of coral patches, extrusions of

pencil coral. On the last dive, I think perhaps this
is my last dive ever in these seas for forty years,
and I see anew the ordinary, the parrotfish,
the butter hamlet, look, the bluehead wrasse. All
is vibrant, new, strange. I do not require dolphins,
as I used to, though they are always very fine: my
eyes dilate to staghorn coral, star coral, orange
tube coral with full attention. Today, I am beside

my friend in hospice. I read to her, uncertain she
hears, her own grave and lucid poems. Old days,
diving, I wore only a bikini and life vest. Why didn't

I shiver back then? Sometimes I was exultant,
sometimes I was scared. This time, I was not frail
underwater but accepted the help through the wild
surf above. Now, through prisms of water, I behold
faces: casts alive with disk and purple leaf corals,

the transmutation of her dear lambent face to ivory,
ours (*mine?*) that will cease from being frail and be
recast as bone and hair and stone and ash and pearl.

INDEPENDENCE DAY 2017

All across the country, dogs are wearing anxiety
wrap Thundershirts and being misted and massaged
with Canine Calm. Across the west, men are wary
of their grills. Seedless personal watermelons,
nervously purchased too soon, have gone punk.
My father, who used to take his three little girls
to the stadium for the intemperate rite of fireworks,
ground and sky, died uncounted on election day.

My husband wears his flag-striped superhero tee-shirt
from Universal Studios. My nod is a blue shirt and red
earrings unseen beneath my hair. Well, and the underpants
are white. Tonight we two will have our burgers, comfort
the pup, sit on the front step to catch the distant fireworks,
and clink our Coronas to each other. These—amidst the noise
and the fire—are our small rituals. Hold me, Captain America.

LIT BLUE SKY FALLING

> *You can no more win a war than you can win an earthquake.*
> —Jeannette Rankin, (1880-1973, first woman elected to
> the U.S. Congress)

Before they were mine, my father
in the uniform held his arm around
my mother in her long black butterfly
dress with built-in falsies. My mother's
best friend married a man headed
for the trenches and got polio and danced
the hitchhiker from her wheelchair. Kids,
they went to the movies on bread-loaf
wrappers and in the dark watched
the sped-up footage of marching
troops. I could never get her to talk
about Nazis, nor my father about his useless
horse troops drilling in a Michigan field
for Germany. Now the last
of my mother's friends sends
a clipping about the awards for war
photography her husband never claimed,
and a photo of herself, white-haired
in her wheelchair, in jeans and a red shirt,
as if she has taken lessons from my dead
mother, and a note: *Yesterday my granddaughter
was over and I said let's draw a picture of what
we see out the window. The river is there
& goes out to Lake Michigan. Amber did hers
like it was summer and docks with boats
in slips. Mine was winter scene
and all the bare trees and docks.*
My father says war is going to happen,
topple, topple, topple. Nothing, not even grief,
is so pure. Vital people live their lives
in wheelchairs, hand-dancing in full
view of winter. A man whose battle
photographs carried the black and white
unglory from blood-soaked field to *Life*
back home could never claim them.
The men of my time hold sealed
boxes of jungle inside their bodies,
and that virulent jungle holds

hooches and flame and snakes
and smoking villes and elephant
grass and the last grenade to blow
open the box at their days' end. All
of our days, across all the rivers
and lakes and oceans, were meant
to be boats carrying us and those we
single out to love past the waving
grasses and beneath the green
canopy, the lit blue sky falling all
around us, and into the slips
at dusk. War, war quakes
all around us, and before us
all the bare trees and docks.

HOW TO TRAVEL WITH YOUR TWIN SISTERS

> *Old Norse, which was once the common language*
> *of all Scandinavia, has branched and modulated*
> *radically in Norway, Sweden, and Denmark....*
> *Icelandic alone remains close to old Norse—so close*
> *that schoolchildren can read medieval classics with ease.*
> —Iceland: Land of the Sagas by David Roberts

Know this land, these mountains by our names
of their colors: brown, gray/green, touched
with rust, black, tan. Gray-milk water courses
through lava rocks. Thermal steam purls from
the ground. On the second night, conduct your
private happy hour with duty-free wine, unfold
your tremulous teenage selves, training bras and
armpits. Touch the ways you saved each other
and failed each other as children when it was
beyond your duty or ability. Bring your mother

back to this earth and name yourselves
Margrétaedóttir. Don't blame her for your tic
heredity. We are ticky, your sister says, and
you know you are the tickiest of all. Collect
facts—the arctic tern flies the equivalent
in migration to the moon, no snakes and few
bugs, reindeer imported, its first inhabitants
literate, Iceland alone lacks a prehistory—
not to recite them back home but only to have
them, like the sheep tucked into fields here.

What is the name of the tiny ground flower
on the lava rocks? Ride the rolls, the mountains
of the rocky land, the treeless still sweeps. Vik is
a bay, fjord is a big bay. Gather them in English:
Bay of the Swans, Fjord of the Ram, Bay of the Polar
Bear, Valley of the Horses, Waterfall of the Sheep Hut.
Climb Helgafell. Scold your sisters for disregarding
the rules about wishes: You do not look back, speak
a word or reveal. You face east. But they know better
than to believe such a story, having their own twin

rules. Listen to your guide: *Do not call the Icelandic*
horses ponies. Three trees make a forest. If you

get lost in the forest, stand up. Try to be still. Go
to the Bay of Childhood, where you are able
to remember your prehistory and now to see
you might choose stillness but require motion.
Fall into sleep on the bus with the comfort
of your sisters' secret twin language behind you,
a medieval language you never knew and now
don't need to know, except that it exists.

SUBLUNARY

> *The last destination isn't the final place
> on the itinerary but what happens when
> we get home and try to make sense of it.*
> —Pico Iyer

We had already planned our trip before
our father died, so we can't say we wanted
to follow him into alien territory. Yet here
we are, with some 120 words for wind, with
cloud shadows striped across hills, in the Rift
Valley where the tectonic plates meet—and
are separating. We walk in blue shoe-covers
in the orange-tan earth of thermal steam. One
sister and I were there at the end, and we try
telling the one who was on the other side
of the world about the repetitive call he made
—letters, it seemed, over and over. *What do
you want, Dad? What do you need? Oh, what?*
Our husbands guessed: I'm ready to go. Here
we go to the sea where the whales rise from
the universal blue. We raise our sisters' arms
in the geothermal seawater of the Blue Lagoon,
and in the photo is a reflection of our alien
bodies. My sister makes the sound of our father

at the end and the absent sister instantly knows:
Margaret. He called her, did he see her? was she
receiving him? And I break into tears. Of course,
of course. I guess you had not to be there to hear
him. I don't know why I believed geology was fixed.
In 1963 new island Surtsey rose from the sea, and
within two years sea rockets grew on the shoreline.
We traverse lava fields to the glacier-covered volcano
Katla striped black and white, its harmonic tremors
presaging another eruption. We enter the chamber
of a black ice cave that looks in my photo for all
the world like my pregnant nieces' sonograms. After
a death, signs appear, the butterfly, the column of light
through clouds, our way to keep a spirit here. Geology
is now. Truth? The signs were always here. And so
the dead teach us how to be awake here in the sublunary

world—these Northern Lights, these tiny purple flowers on the lava rock by the waterfall, this small shaggy horse. We are Haraldsdóttir, returned home.

TRANSLATION OF BONES

The National Museum of Iceland

(when the worldly remains of a saint are removed from the earth and then set in a casket and considered to be a holy relic of the Church)
—Armann Jakobsson, *Icelandic Literature of the Vikings*

I understand bone as a kind of metonym for the soul.
—Gina Franco

In a glass case a Viking skeleton unearthed
from a pagan grave rests—in just the shape
of my own sleep. I buy the best replica
of the bronze Thor, seated, helmeted, hands
clasping his hammer or a cross or both, forged
after all in the year 1000. Our father's body
passed more than a thousand miles across
six states, carried from hospice bed to
mausoleum's top row beside our mother.
In Njal's Saga, Svanur entered the mountain
when he died, another kind of translation.
At Althing in 1000 AD, pagan priest Þorgeir
brooded for a day and a night, silent under
his furs, and then interpreted his prayer

(to whom?): *the land would be consecrated
Christian. No horsemeat. Here is the new
White God. Thursday, Thor's Day, is now
Fimmtudagur, Fifth Day. What you beg Thor
in the tempest no one cares.* My husband,
after all the unforgivable deaths, will not call
out. Damn you, Odin, he says. And now
we three sisters here at Góðafoss record
the sluice and the rainbow and the sweep
of this three-sided Waterfall of the Gods.

Here the Lawmaker threw over the old gods.
Perhaps there were three trees in the low
sky. The literature says he "disposed of,"
"abandoned," and "honored" them. I see
him manhandling the superhuman-sized

wood carvings to the falls. I see him
alone. He pushes one-eyed Odin, then
Thor gripping Mjölnir, then Frey into
the cascade. Two ravens break from
Odin's shoulders and are flung into
the sky. Thus are the gods taken from
the land and given to the water. I wear
my Sleipnir tee-shirt, my miniature Thor
rests on my desk. Thus are bones lofted
from earth to tomb, relics beyond gravity.
In my mind I turn our father in his case
sideways to his familiar sleep pose, and
memory settles with bright wings upon us.

AURORA BOREALIS

> *Smiling while dying is apparently not that unusual. The body tries to produce a state of euphoria to usher us out. It releases the same kinds of neurochemicals, dopamine and serotonin, that flood our brains as we are falling in love.*
> —Edwidge Danticat

In truth, the only reason I wanted to go to Iceland was for the Northern Lights. They shimmer on others of our parent star, Jupiter, Saturn, but that does me no good. Here the annulus is the band centered around the magnetic pole. Solar winds blow the showers of particles along our magnetic fields. But it's art I desire, not science. Freud said we aren't able to believe mortality because we can't imagine ourselves absent. Ah. The lights happen even when we can't see them. Likely the Vikings wouldn't have seen them. Dark is required. On

the second night, we bundle up and settle behind the Stykkishólmskirkja Church, though we don't see its whale vertebra shape and its Madonna who is a blue aurora herself until morning. The lights begin, silken plumes and arcs and sheets, and we sit beneath these moving green ghosts. At last, as they fade in the cold, the poet and the painter take their table arts inside, and know the many other reasons for their Iceland, but the photographer waits in the exultant green/dark. She is all of us at the end, I want to think, elusive, in love, and still present beneath green glory.

SKALD

> *Young were the years when Ymir made his settlement, there was no sand nor sea nor cool waves, earth was nowhere nor the sky above, chaos yawned, grass was there nowhere.*
> From "Seeress's Prophecy," *Prose Edda*, Snorri Sturluson, translated by Carolyne Larrington

While Europe erected castles, Iceland made
sagas. Between covers of sealskin, lambskin
pages of feuds, magic, and fate—oh, Njal must
go to his burning—coolly deliver the brutal
details of art. The poet was esteemed among
Vikings, chanting of the twilight of the gods, earth's
rebirth, praise of the kings, and still the country
subsidizes its poets. The craft is intricate: metres,

syllables, kennings, *heiti*. In the sagas, the world
was enchanted, with no salvation from the world
but glory in the earth. Did they make the poems
to sing the counterpoint of love, grief, the brutal
details? Flying home, we observe the stretched sky's
white/gray jagged clouds scattered like icebergs,
the sullen earth receiving the cast shadows—
art floating above the reality, or perhaps the shadows

are the art. Or not reflection but travel from home
to a secret destination that is both arrival and end.
From above, the black cliffs brim into the sea, the neat
hem of the past ravels into our present, the horizon
blurs. Ice giant Ymir, first being, was born into darkness
over the surface of the deep, but then demarcations
began—light and dark, vault and water, land and sea.
Now, over the sea, the clouds blend to a blurred sheet.

And is this why we make art? to blur the lines? Ymir's
land was ravaged and sank back into the sea. Yes,
the story is more complicated than that, isn't it now,
and I like to believe that Njal could have turned from
his burning, that life and death shade into each other.
A new green world rose from the sea. And here we
three sisters cast our small visions into the grass
that is everywhere, oh everywhere, and always.

Meg Files is the author of the novels *Meridian 144* and *The Third Law of Motion, Home Is the Hunter and Other Stories, The Love Hunter and Other Poems,* and *Writing What You Know,* a book about using personal experience and taking risks with writing. She edited *Lasting: Poems on Aging*. Her awards include a Bread Loaf Fellowship. She taught creative writing, directed the Pima Writers' Workshop, and chaired the English and Journalism Department at Pima College for many years. She was the James Thurber Writer-in-Residence at The Ohio State University and the Doris Leadbetter Writer-in-Residence at Victoria University in Australia. She directs the Tucson Festival of Books Literary Awards and Masters Workshop.

www.ingramcontent.com/pod-product-compliance
Lightning Source LLC
LaVergne TN
LVHW041602070426
835507LV00011B/1254